· brought to

MICRO PEAS

· THE SERIES ·

danielle renov

RENA MAUSKOPF
photographer
graphic design

PENINA RUBIN
production and
operations

NATASHA HAIMOVICH
prop stylist

First Edition — First Impression / November 2024

Published by **ARTSCROLL / SHAAR PRESS**
313 Regina Avenue / Rahway, NJ / 07065
(718) 921-9000 / www.artscroll.com

Distributed in Israel by **SIFRIATI / A. GITLER**
POB 2351 / Bnei Brak 51122 / Israel / 03-579-8187

Distributed in Europe by **LEHMANNS**
Unit E, Viking Business Park, Rolling Mill Road
Jarrow, Tyne and Wear, NE32 3DP / England

Distributed in Australia and New Zealand by
GOLDS WORLD OF JUDAICA
3-13 William Street / Balaclava, Melbourne 3183, Victoria / Australia

Distributed in South Africa by **KOLLEL BOOKSHOP**
Northfield Centre / 17 Northfield Avenue
Glenhazel 2192 / Johannesburg, South Africa

ISBN-10: 1-4226-4196-1 / ISBN-13: 978-1-4226-4196-5

Printed in PRC

dedication

This book is dedicated to Hakadosh Baruch Hu.
I try every day to live my life in a way that
honors Him and His Torah.

May this book serve as a vehicle to illuminate
His glory throughout the world.

To Eli, and our children in both worlds,
Yechezkel Meir, Yisroel Dov, Leah Baila,
Shifra Batya, Margalit Bracha, Yaakov Rafael z"l,
Elisheva Tova, Efrat Tehilla and Chaya Roiza,
everything I do is for you.
I feel blessed every day that I get to
call you my family.

May the berachos (blessings) said on the
food cooked from these recipes
be a zechus for our son,
Yaakov Rafael z"l ben Eliyahu Yerachmiel n"y.

acknowledgments

Before anything, I thank **Hashem** for everything He has bestowed upon me. Nothing would be possible without Him and I am so grateful every day.

To **Eli**, I am so grateful to have you by my side. Your unwavering support, love and belief in me is the driving force behind everything I do. Thanks for choosing me!

To **my children**, thanks for being the best taste testers and cheerleaders a mother could ask for. I couldn't do any of this without all of your love and support.

To my parents, **Nicole** and **Marc Gleitman**, my kids learned how to cheer me on from your example. Thanks for always believing in me and supporting me! You are the ultimate hype team!

To my in-laws, **Ruki** and **Kal Renov**, thank you for being the best in-laws and grandparents. Eli, our kids and I are so lucky to have you.

To **Rena Mauskopf**, **Penina Rubin** and **David Herskowitz** thank you for all your hard work. Adding you all to the Peas Love & Carrots team was the best professional decision I've ever made! MICRO PEAS would not have happened without you!

Udeni Karunanayaka, **Rachel Dimerman** and **Yisroel Cohen**, your hard work and support helps me juggle all the the tasks needed to manage a busy household, family and work.

Joyce Ehrlich and **Vicki Isakow**, thank you for being the best prep cooks! You ensured that the food was prepped to perfection and because of you both, the whole photo shoot went off without a hitch.

Natasha Haimovich, thank you for helping to set the perfect scene for each photo. I appreciate all your hard work and attention to detail.

To **Barbara** and **Bob Deutsch** and **Rachel Shapiro**, thank you for the constant edits. Your listening ear and helpful comments made the writing fun.

To **BENNY'S MEAT SHOP**, thank you for the many years of providing my family with the cleanest, most delicious chicken and meat to be found in Israel. Special thanks for providing all of the beautiful chicken highlighted in the photos. Contact Benny's at their website **bennys.co.il** or via WhatsApp **+972 29955888**.

Thank you to all of the **recipe testers** from all over the world who made sure that each recipe turned into its best possible version...
Shmuel Baumser, Ahuva Blumenfeld, Lauren Bochner, Sara Bodenheim, Randy Cohen, Esther Dana, Meredith Deutsch-Levy, Maddie Dickstein, Lorraine Domb, Danielle Dweck, Randi Feitelberg, Chaya Freedman, Sara Friedman, Shirley Friedman, Dini Goldring, Shaina Gordon, Sara Gorodetsky, Ahuva Greenbaum, Shayna Chaya Greenfield, Laura Grella, Leeba Grunstein, Sheri Hammer, Sabrina Harari, Rifkey Isseroff, Naomi Karon, Miriam Kattan, Hindy Katz, Amy Krausz, Elisa Levi, Rachel Licht, Fredda Loewenstein, Sara Margolies, Michele Meiner, Esther Moser, Shira Moskovitz, Shaindee Moskowitz, Frimmy Muller, Andrea Raisin, Vivi Rosenberg, Suzie Sayegy, Liala Schnell, Jessica Sosnovich, Shoshana Sova, Yona Sternstein, Avital Vogel, Sora Wahrhaftig, Jessica Weiss

introduction

IT WAS WITHIN days of my first cookbook hitting the shelves that people began to ask me when the second volume was coming out. Never. That was my answer over and over again. The fact that I'm sitting here typing another introduction is a testament to my love of fine-tuning and sharing recipes with each one of you.

See, writing a cookbook was one of the great experiences of my life. Yes, it comes with a lot of computer time — not my thing — but it also comes along with a creative process unlike any other. Each part of the book offers a unique artistic avenue of expression. Developing the recipes, setting the scene for the photo, taking the photo and playing with light, exploring the world of typography and graphic design are all a part of the journey a cookbook author takes. I relished every minute of it.

At the same time, it is incredibly time consuming. Like all art forms it consumes you. Once I was done with the first book I couldn't see how to possibly commit to that kind of process again.

And then, at the very moment that I was so sure I would never write a cookbook again, Hashem provided me with the inspiration and desire and, well, here we are. Not writing a traditional cookbook, but writing our redefined and upgraded version.

So, what happened? A year or two back I needed a recipe for something and had to search through so many cookbooks and online recipes to find one that appealed to me. All I kept thinking was that I wished there was a an entire book just dedicated to this one item. And thus, THE MICRO PEAS SERIES was born.

Often I start my cooking with an ingredient or idea. I have a package of chicken I need to use, I need a recipe for a bundt cake, I want to serve fish but am tired of my usual recipes... All typical thoughts that occur in a regular home kitchen when cooking happens daily. We just want someone we trust to lay out all our options in one place, with recipes and (pretty) photos so that we can choose quickly and easily.

That is what the MICRO PEAS SERIES is all about. A micro (in size, not awesomeness) cookbook featuring one very specific ingredient or idea. The goal is to put out loads of these, each with its own topic to meet all of our different needs. This enables you to buy those that speak to you at an affordable price, skip the ones that don't, and enjoy easy and clear access to the recipes you need.

From the moment this idea popped into my mind, I fell in love. Being able to immerse myself in the zprocess in small bursts of time and bring you no-fail, trusted, delicious and affordable recipes in an easier format is a dream for me. Not to mention that each book will take on a life of its own based on its niche topic or ingredient, allowing me a new creative avenue so that none of this ever gets stale!

Food is the vehicle through which I connect to people. I love nothing more than sitting around a delicious table chatting and connecting to those I am with. It is my love language.

My hope is that the recipes on these pages will bring us all to the table, break down the walls that exist among us and open the lines of communication in order to facilitate acceptance, connection with each other and create meaningful relationships.

May all our prayers be answered with revealed goodness and may we be blessed with health, happiness and peace. May we merit to greet Mashiach Tzidkeinu speedily and in our days, Amen selah.

Happy cooking,

things to know

	METRIC SYSTEM	AVOIRDUPOIS SYSTEM google it!	APPROXIMATE NUMBER OF PIECES
boneless chicken breast	400-600 grams	.88-1.322 pounds	1
	1 kilo	2.2	4
thin chicken cutlet	66 grams	0.14 pounds	1
	1 kilo	2.2	15
boneless skinless chicken thigh	110 grams	0.24 pounds	1
	1.1 kilo	2.42	10

- It is fine if the weight of your chicken is a few grams or ounces more or less than specified in the recipe.
- All of these recipes specify chicken breast or chicken thigh. In every recipe you can actually swap them easily if you adjust the cooking times.
- Boneless chicken breasts cooks more quickly than boneless chicken thighs.
- Black pepper is always coarse black pepper.
- Salt is always kosher salt unless otherwise specified.
- Granulated spices are coarser than their powdered counterparts.
- Olive oil is always extra virgin olive oil.
- Neutral oil can be avocado, canola, grapeseed, safflower, peanut or any other oil with little to no flavor and generally have a higher smoking point. My favorite is avocado!
- All cooking times in this book are according to the temperatures given. If a recipe is supposed to cook on medium high heat and you cook it on high heat, the outside will burn before the item is cooked all the way through to the center.

A NOTE ON SPICES AND HERBS

- Many recipes in this book call for fresh herbs.
- If you want to replace fresh herbs with dried herbs, please be mindful to adjust the amounts. 1 Tablespoon of freshly chopped cilantro does NOT equal 1 Tablespoon of dried cilantro.
- I prefer fresh herbs; however, sometimes dried herbs must happen. When using dried herbs, measure out what you need, then place them in the palms of your hands and gently rub them to help release their flavors before adding to the dish.

1 tsp dried herbs = 1 Tbsp fresh herbs

breakdown of a chicken

for the purpose of this book

contents

WHITE MEAT:

greek chicken salad 10
chicken fajitas 16
caesar chicken pinwheels 20
chopped chicken salad 26
lemon herb skillet chicken 30
chicken cacciatore 32
sticky chicken pastrami hash 34
chicken and broccoli 36
one pot chicken and ptitim 40
general tso chicken 42

DARK MEAT:

chimichurri-ish grilled pargiyot 12
stewed chicken ktzitzot 14
shawarma chicken bake with roasted garlic techina 18
moroccan chicken and sweet potato tagine 22
broiled buffalo chicken wraps 24
loaded chicken borekas 28
sheet pan dijon chicken and potatoes 38

dum dum dum the plot chickens

greek chicken salad

I LOVE A SALAD THAT CAN PASS FOR A WHOLE MEAL OR BE SERVED FAMILY STYLE ALONGSIDE A BUNCH OF OTHER DISHES. EVERYTHING ABOUT THIS SALAD IS YUMMY. THE CHICKEN IS JUICY AND PACKED WITH FLAVOR, THE DRESSING IS SLURP WORTHY AND THE RECIPE CAN BE MIXED AND MATCHED TO SUIT YOUR NEEDS. NEED A GREAT GRILLED CHICKEN? JUST MAKE THE CHICKEN! WANT TO STUFF EVERYTHING INTO PITAS OR ROLLS? GO FOR IT!

CHICKEN:

8 thin chicken cutlets

3 Tbsp olive oil

5 cloves garlic, minced

1 tsp kosher salt

½ tsp black pepper

½ tsp dried oregano

2 Tbsp fresh lemon juice

1 Tbsp red wine vinegar

DRESSING:

2 lemons, juiced

1 Tbsp red wine vinegar

2 tsp kosher salt

1 tsp dried parsley

½ tsp black pepper

1 cup olive oil

Put in a jar and shake well to combine.

SALAD:

4 cups gently torn romaine leaves

4 Persian cucumbers, sliced in half lengthwise, seeds removed, cut into ¼ inch half-moons

1 red pepper, diced

1 purple onion, finely minced

1 tomato, diced

1 cup pitted kalamata olives, halved

2 cups shredded white or purple cabbage

1 grilled hot pepper, sliced/minced (see below)

1 cup slightly crushed pita chips (optional)

Serves 6

CHICKEN:
Combine everything in a bowl. Mix well to coat. Heat grill pan on medium high heat. Grill for about 2 min on each side. Chicken can be made 1-2 days in advance and sliced cold into the salad.

HOT PEPPERS:
Put as many as you want in a bowl. Drizzle 1 tsp **olive oil** and sprinkle 1 tsp **kosher salt**. Add to hot grill. Char on all sides. You only need 1 for this recipe but I love having them in my fridge to add to salads and sandwiches. Store airtight container for up to 10 days.

ASSEMBLE:
Layer all the vegetables on a large platter. Slice chicken cutlets into thin strips and place over the vegetables.
Sprinkle **pita chips** on top if using.
Drizzle dressing over everything.
Serve and enjoy!

chimichurri-ish grilled pargiyot

I WOULD CALL THIS AN ALL PURPOSE CHICKEN BECAUSE YOU CAN SLICE IT INTO ANY SALAD, SERVE IT OVER RICE OR COUSCOUS, IN A SANDWICH OR EAT IT JUST AS IS! THE CHIMICHURRI IS PACKED WITH FLAVOR AND IS JUST AS DELICIOUS BRUSHED OVER GRILLED VEGGIES OR A PIECE OF FISH AS IT IS ON CHICKEN!

Yields 10 pieces

CHIMICHURRI:

1½ cup cilantro leaves

2 scallions, washed and dried

2 cloves garlic, peeled

1 tsp dijon mustard

1 Tbsp red wine vinegar

1 lemon, juiced

2 tsp kosher salt

1 tsp black pepper

1 tsp crushed red pepper flakes (optional)

3 Tbsp olive oil

10 boneless, skinless chicken thighs

The chimichurri is great as a marinade or dip for any protein.

Place **cilantro**, **scallions**, **garlic**, **mustard**, **vinegar**, **lemon juice**, **salt**, **pepper** and **crushed red pepper** in the bowl of a food processor. Pulse until everything is finely chopped. At the last second drizzle in **oil** until just combined. Place mixture into a bowl.

In a medium sized bowl add **chicken** and 4 Tbsp of the **chimichuri mixture**. Mix to combine. Allow to marinate for 10 minutes and no more than 30 minutes.

Heat a grill or place a grill pan over medium high heat. Lightly grease and add a few pieces of chicken at a time, being careful not to overcrowd the pan.

Cook for 6 minutes on the first side, flip and right away brush the cooked side with a small dollop of the remaining chimichurri mixture.

Cook second side for 4 minutes, flip, brush second side with a dollop of chimichurri mixture, flip again just so the chimichurri heats through for 10 seconds and remove from pan.

That's confusing. Let's break it down... Basically, you're cooking both sides completely, adding a little extra mixture to each side and cooking both sides again for 10-20 seconds.

Serve hot or cold, slice into a salad, alongside roasted vegetables, or in a wrap or sandwich and enjoy!

stewed chicken ktzitzot

"GAN" FOOD BUT MAKE IT DINNER AND DELICIOUS!

Serves 6

CHICKEN:

1 kilo (2.2 lb) ground dark meat chicken

½ cup cilantro leaves

2 cloves garlic

1 yellow onion, halved

1 Tbsp kosher salt

1 tsp black pepper

1 egg, beaten

1½ cups plain breadcrumbs

2 Tbsp neutral oil

SAUCE:

1 Tbsp neutral oil

1 large yellow onion, halved, thinly sliced

2 tsp kosher salt

½ tsp black pepper

2 cloves garlic, minced

2 Tbsp tomato paste

2 tsp paprika

1 tsp turmeric

1 bag frozen artichoke hearts, thawed, any rough pieces removed, halved (optional)

¼ cup dry red wine

1 15oz can tomato sauce

2 cups chicken stock (or water)

1 cup frozen peas

In the bowl of a food processor, add **cilantro leaves**, **garlic**, **onion halves**, **salt** and **pepper**. Blend until everything is finely chopped.

Add mixture to a large bowl along with **ground chicken**, **egg** and **breadcrumbs**. Mix until well combined. Remove 2 Tbsp at a time and form into a "meatball." Place on a piece of parchment and repeat until the chicken mixture is finished.

Heat a pot over medium high heat.
Add 2 Tbsp **oil** and a batch of the chicken balls, being careful not to overcrowd the pot. Sear for 2 minutes and then gently rotate to cook on another side. I usually sear them on 3 sides to keep the roundish shape. Remove from pot and repeat until all the chicken balls are seared. You may need to add an extra 1 Tbsp of oil between batches. Set aside.

Using the same pot the chicken was cooked in, add **oil**, **onion**, **salt** and **pepper**. Cook for 15 minutes, stirring often.

Add **garlic**, **tomato paste**, **paprika**, **turmeric** and **artichoke hearts**, if using, to the pot. Stir constantly for 3 minutes.

Add in **wine**, use a wooden spoon to scrape up any bits from the bottom of the pot. Cook for 2 minutes to reduce wine.

Add in **tomato sauce** and **chicken stock**. Return chicken balls to the pot and add **peas**, stir to combine. Bring mixture to a boil, reduce heat to low, cover the pot and cook for 1 hour, stirring every 15-20 minutes. If after 35-40 minutes the sauce is drying out (this can happen if your stove is a bit hotter than mine!) add an additional ½ cup of **water**. Serve hot, alongside rice or couscous, in a pita or enjoy as is!

Don't have artichokes?
Leave out or replace
with other veggies like
string beans, peppers,
zucchini...

chicken fajitas

TRADITIONALLY FAJITAS ARE SERVED IN CORN OR FLOUR TORTILLAS WITH ALL THE TRIMMINGS AS SHOWN IN THE PHOTO BUT THESE FAJITAS ARE SO FLAVORFUL THEY ARE JUST AS GOOD SERVED OVER RICE. SOMETIMES I EVEN SERVE IT OVER A SWEET POTATO, BAKED POTATO STYLE!

Serves 8-10

12 thin chicken cutlets, cut into ¼ inch strips

4 Tbsp olive oil, divided

4 Tbsp Maggie Loves Taco Spice Blend (or your favorite taco seasoning)

2 yellow onions, halved, thinly sliced

2 red bell peppers, cut into thin strips

1 jalapeño, minced

4 cloves garlic, minced

1 chipotle in adobo + **1 Tbsp** adobo sauce

1 cup light beer

1 cup water

½ cup cilantro leaves, chopped

OPTIONAL:

10 tortillas

1-2 limes, cut into wedges

1 avocado, thinly sliced or guacamole

1 small bunch of cilantro

Place **chicken** in a bowl with 1 Tbsp **oil** and 1 Tbsp **spice blend**. Mix, set aside. This can be done the night before and placed in the fridge to marinate.

Preheat a large pan over medium high heat.

Add 2 Tbsp of **olive oil** and all the chicken. Cook, stirring often until the chicken is cooked through, about 6 minutes. Remove chicken from the pan and set aside.

Add remaining **oil** along with **onions, peppers** and **jalapeño**. Cook for 15 minutes stirring every few minutes. Mix in 2 Tbsp of **spice blend** and **garlic**. Cook for 2 minutes.

Return chicken to the pan along with **chipotle**, **adobo sauce** and remaining **spice blend**. Stir to combine.

Add **beer** into pan and use a wooden spoon to scrape up any bits from the bottom of the pan. Allow mixture to cook for 5 minutes and then add **water**. Stir, reduce heat to low and cover the pan. Cook for another 20 minutes. Remove from heat and add chopped cilantro.

Serve any way you like and enjoy!

Depending on the brand of taco spice blend you used, you may need to add a bit more salt, so taste it and adjust to your liking!

shawarma chicken bake with roasted garlic techina

SOMETIMES YOU WANT THAT ISRAELI SHAWARMA FLAVOR AND YOU JUST WANT IT TO APPEAR MAGICALLY. WELL, HERE YOU GO. A COMPLETE SHAWARMA STYLE DINNER MADE ON A SINGLE BAKING SHEET. THE ONLY BIT OF "EXTRA" HERE IS THE TECHINA AND EVEN THAT WORK IS MINIMAL. THIS IS THE PERFECT DINNER OR SHABBOS DAY DISH WHEN YOU WANT SOMETHING EASY BUT WOW!

CHICKEN:

8 boneless skinless chicken thighs

2 Tbsp olive oil

3 Tbsp shawarma spice blend

1 lemon, juiced

Serves 4-6

VEGETABLES:

1 yellow onion, peeled, halved and thinly sliced

2 cups frozen cauliflower florets, thawed

1 medium sweet potato, peeled, cut into 1 inch cubes

1 cup frozen string beans

2 Tbsp olive oil

2 tsp kosher salt

1 tsp black pepper

1 tsp paprika

1 tsp granulated garlic

2 tsp granulated onion

ROASTED GARLIC TECHINA:

1 whole garlic bulb, top cut off just to expose top of the cloves

1 tsp olive oil

2¼ tsp kosher salt, divided

½ cup tahini paste

1 lemon, juiced

1⅓ cups cold water, divided

Preheat oven to 200°C (400°F) and line a baking sheet with parchment paper.

In a large bowl combine **all the ingredients** for the **chicken** and mix well. Marinate for up to 1 hour. Lay chicken out on one half of the baking sheet. (They can be smushed together.)

In the same bowl you used for the chicken add **all the ingredients** for the **vegetables**. Mix well to combine. Pour onto the other half of the baking sheet, spreading into a single layer as much as possible.

Place **garlic bulb** for the techina in a small piece of tin foil. Drizzle **olive oil** and sprinkle ¼ tsp **salt** over the exposed cloves. Wrap loosely and place in a corner of the baking sheet.

Place baking sheet into the oven and cook for 1 hour.
After 45 minutes remove the garlic and if the chicken is cooked to your satisfaction, you can remove it from the tray as well and allow the vegetables to continue cooking.

Meanwhile make the techina.
Squeeze the bulb of roasted garlic to release the inner cloves into the food processor along with **tahini paste**, **lemon** and **salt**. Blend. While blending, drizzle in 1 cup of **cold water**. If mixture is too thick you can add 1 Tbsp more at a time from the remaining ⅓ cup. Once the techina is your desired consistency store in an airtight container for up to 10 days.

Remove baking sheet from the oven, place all the roasted veggies on a serving dish. Add chicken on top and drizzle a few Tablespoons of **techina** over the top.
Serve hot (or cold). Leftovers make excellent lunches! Enjoy!

caesar chicken pinwheel skewers

THIS DISH COMES TOGETHER QUICKLY AND IS THE PERFECT RECIPE TO GET YOUR KIDS INVOLVED. IT'S VERSATILE, APROCHABLE AND, IN MY EXPERIENCE, IF IT COMES ON A STICK, KIDS WILL EAT IT.

Yields 30 pinwheels

12 thin chicken cutlets (thin is key here!)

6 (8 inch) flour tortillas

20 wooden skewers

2 tbsp neutral oil

CAESAR MAYO:

⅔ cup mayonnaise

¼ cup dijon mustard

1 lemon, juiced

2 tsp fish-free Worcestershire sauce

2 tsp red wine vinegar

6 cloves garlic, minced

1 Tbsp kosher salt

1 tsp black pepper

If your chicken cutlets are a drop thicker than the ones we used, you may find they need a bit more time to cook. In that case, grill as directed and then place on a baking sheet and into a preheated 175°C (350°F) oven for 8-12 minutes to cook through.

Immerse **skewers** in cold water in a rimmed dish.

In a medium bowl add all the **caesar mayo ingredients** and mix to combine.

Lay **tortillas** out on counter. Smear each tortilla with a thin layer of the **caesar mayo mixture**.

Add 2 thin **chicken cutlets** onto each tortilla, arranging them so that they mostly cover the entire tortilla in one single layer.

Brush the top of the chicken with a little more of the caesar mayo mixture.
Roll up each tortilla pinwheel style. Slice each roll into 5 equal pieces.

Holding 2 skewers together, insert through pinwheel from the side (see photo) to keep pinwheels sealed.

Place 3 pinwheels on each pair of skewers. (Two skewers add more stability when flipping them on the grill). Repeat until you have 10 sets of skewers with 3 pinwheels on each.

Brush the surface of the pinwheels with **oil**.

Preheat grill or grill pan to medium high heat and lightly grease. Place skewers on the grill, cook for 3-4 minutes on all four sides. Serve hot and enjoy!

Get creative with your flavors here! Swap out caesar mayo for pesto, barbecue sauce, or whatever you are in the mood for!

If your tortillas are larger, you will need to put 3 pieces on each wrap and will need a total of 18 chicken cutlets.

moroccan chicken and sweet potato tagine

POV: THERE'S A CHILL IN THE AIR AND IT'S BEEN RAINING ON AND OFF ALL DAY. THE SUN SETS EARLY, AND EVERYONE WALKS INTO THE HOUSE WHEN IT'S ALREADY DARK. AS THEY OPEN THE DOOR THEY'RE IMMEDIATELY HIT WITH BEAUTIFUL WARMING AROMAS OF THIS SLOW COOKED TAGINE. THEY THROW DOWN THEIR JACKETS, WASH UP AND YOU HAND THEM A BOWL OF COUSCOUS WITH A PIPING HOT LADLE OF THIS TAGINE. MMMMM.

Serves 6-8

8 boneless, skinless, chicken thighs, cut into 1-2 inch cube like pieces

3 Tbsp olive oil, divided

2 yellow onions, peeled, halved, thinly sliced

1 leek, halved, thinly sliced, washed, dried

3 tsp kosher salt, divided

1 tsp black pepper

4 cloves garlic, minced

1 inch piece ginger, grated

2 Tbsp tomato paste

2-3 tsp harissa (or any chili paste you like), optional but recommended

1 tsp turmeric

1 tsp paprika

1 sweet potato, peeled, quartered lengthwise, cut into 1 inch cubes

¼ cup dry white wine

1 can chickpeas, drained and rinsed well

2 cups chicken stock (or water)

Heat a large heavy bottom pot over medium high heat.

Add 2 Tbsp **oil**, **onions**, **leek**, 1 tsp **salt** and **pepper** to the pot. Cook for 20 minutes, uncovered, stirring often.

Move onions to the outer edges of the pot and add remaining 1 Tbsp **oil** and **chicken** to the center of the pot. Sprinkle remaining **salt** over the chicken.

Allow the chicken to cook for 2 minutes. Then stirring slowly, incorporate the onions and leeks with the chicken.

Once chicken is cooked through, add **garlic**, **ginger**, **tomato paste**, **harissa**, **turmeric** and **paprika** to the pot. Cook for 2 minutes, stirring constantly, to allow flavors to deepen.

Add **sweet potato**, stir to combine.
Add in **wine**. Using a wooden spoon, scrape up any bits from the bottom of the pot.

Add **chickpeas** and **stock**. Bring to a boil, then reduce heat to low, cover the pot and allow to simmer for 60-90 minutes, stirring gently every so often.

Depending on whether you used stock or water you may need to add a touch more salt. Once cooked, give it a quick taste and adjust if needed!

Serve hot over a bowl of couscous or rice and enjoy!

Feel free to add in or swap for any vegetables you have on hand, like carrots, celery, fennel, cauliflower, zucchini...

Great make ahead dish-bring to room temperature, then reheat over a low flame, stirring often to distribute heat for about 35 minutes until piping hot!

broiled buffalo chicken wraps

SOMETIMES I JUST WANT THAT BUFFALO POPPER FLAVOR WITHOUT ALL THE EXTRA WORK OF BREADING AND FRYING. I CAME UP WITH THESE AND NOW THIS IS A WEEKLY STAPLE IN MY HOUSE. ALL THE FLAVOR IS THERE, YOU GET THE CRUNCH FROM THE CHARRED WRAP AND VEGGIES AND IT'S ALL NEATLY PACKAGED IN A PORTABLE MEAL VERSION!

Serves 8-10

CHICKEN:

8 boneless, skinless chicken thighs

1 cup buffalo style hot sauce (I use Frank's)

¾ cup maple syrup

SAUCE:

1 cup mayonnaise

1 Tbsp dijon mustard

1 clove garlic, minced

2 tsp fish-free Worcestershire sauce

1 Tbsp dried parsley

2 tsp granulated onion

2 tsp red wine vinegar

WRAPS:

8-10 flour tortillas

4 cups shredded iceberg lettuce

1 large tomato, thinly sliced

4 sour pickles, cut lengthwise into spears

Add anything you like to include in your wraps (sautéed onions, coleslaw, sliced radishes, scallions, marinated jalapeños, eggplant...)

Set oven to low/medium broil setting and lightly grease a baking dish. Place **chicken**, **buffalo sauce** and **maple syrup** in the dish. Mix well to combine. Place in the oven, uncovered for 20 minutes, flipping once halfway through.

While the chicken is cooking, add **all the sauce ingredients** to a bowl and mix well to combine. Store in an airtight container in the fridge for up to 3 weeks.

ASSEMBLE:

Lightly char each **wrap** over an open flame by holding it with tongs and rotating it over the fire for 35 seconds on each side.

Slice each piece of **chicken** into ½ inch strips. Return to baking dish so they can soak up more of that yummy buffalo sauce!

Place a large dollop of sauce in the center of the wrap. Add veggies and whatever other fun stuff you have in your fridge, then top with a few slices of your chicken. Fold in the bottom of the wrap and then roll it up. I like to cover the bottom of each wrap with a small piece of foil so its easier to eat!

Serve and enjoy!

If you can't char the wrap over an open flame, you can fill your tortilla and then place it on a hot, lightly oiled pan for 1 minute on each side to create a panini style wrap.

chopped chicken salad

I LOVE A GOOD SALAD AND THIS JUST HAS EVERY FLAVOR I WANT TO EAT ALL THE TIME. IT'S LIGHT, FRESH, FILLING, SAVORY AND SO INSANELY DELICIOUS. IF I COULD HANDLE EATING CHICKEN IN THE MIDDLE OF THE DAY, I WOULD EAT THIS FOR LUNCH EVERY SINGLE DAY. ALSO, THE BEST PART IS IF YOU SAVE A LITTLE IN A CONAINER FOR THE NEXT DAY, IT WILL STILL BE DELICIOUS!

CHICKEN:

8 thin chicken cutlets

2 tsp olive oil

1 tsp sesame oil

2 cloves garlic, minced

½ inch piece ginger, grated

2 Tbsp soy sauce

Serves 8-10

DRESSING:

¼ cup fresh lime juice (about 3-4 limes)

1 clove garlic, minced

1 Tbsp white miso

2 Tbsp soy sauce

2 Tbsp balsamic vinegar

1 tsp sesame oil

¼ cup neutral oil

2 Tbsp maple syrup (optional; I like it on the more acidic side, so I leave out!)

SALAD:

8-10 stalks kale, shredded

1 head baby bok choy (about 6 leaves), each leaf halved lengthwise, then thinly sliced

½ of a small purple cabbage, finely shredded

2 Persian cucumbers, washed, halved, seeds scraped out, thinly sliced

3 scallions, very thinly sliced

1 shallot, peeled, halved, thinly sliced

1 red chili, minced (optional)

½ cup salted roasted peanuts, chopped

1 tsp sesame seeds

Place **all the ingredients** for the **chicken** into a bowl. Mix to combine. Preheat grill pan over medium high heat. Add chicken in batches and cook for 2-3 minutes on each side.

Place all the **dressing ingredients** in a jar or tight container. Shake well to combine. Place in fridge for up to 10 days. Shake before using.

To serve the salad, add **kale** to a large bowl. Add 2 Tbsp of the **dressing** and using your hands gently massage the dressing into the kale. Add **bok choy**, **cabbage**, **cucumbers**, **scallions**, **shallot** and **chili** to the bowl. Slice **chicken** into thin strips and add to the bowl along with 3 more Tbsp of **dressing**. Mix to combine (taste and add more dressing if you like)! Sprinkle chopped **peanuts** and **sesame seeds** over the top, serve and enjoy!

loaded chicken borekas

EVERYTHING ABOUT THIS CHICKEN BOREKA IS DELICIOUS. THE DIP...YUM! THE CHICKEN MIXTURE...OH MY GOSH! I WRAPPED IT ALL UP IN AN EASY TO SERVE BOREKA. I'VE EVEN MADE IT INTO ONE LONG ROLL AND SOMETIMES JUST SERVE THE CHICKEN MIXTURE PLAIN OVER RICE OR CHUMMUS. IT'S NOT TOO SPICY AT ALL AND JUST PACKED WITH CROWD PLEASING FLAVORFUL YUMMINESS. A GREAT DISH TO ADD TO YOUR DINNER OR SHABBOS COOKING ROTATION!

FILLING:

6 boneless skinless chicken thighs, cut into 1 inch pieces

4 Tbsp olive oil, divided

1 Tbsp + 1 tsp kosher salt, divided

1 tsp black pepper

2 tsp paprika

1 tsp sumac

2 tsp granulated onion

1 tsp granulated garlic

1 tsp turmeric

2 large yellow onions, halved, thinly sliced

1 jalapeño, halved lengthwise, thinly sliced (optional)

¼ cup dry white wine

Yields 24 borekas

BOREKAS:

1 roll (or 2 sheets) puff pastry, defrosted (or 24 precut puff pastry squares)

1 egg, lightly beaten

DIP:

1 cup mayonnaise

3 Tbsp prepared schug

1 lemon, juiced

½ tsp kosher salt

In a bowl, add **chicken** pieces, 1 Tbsp **oil**, 1 Tbsp **salt**, **pepper**, **paprika**, **sumac**, **granulated onion**, **granulated garlic** and **turmeric**. Mix until well combined. Marinate for 30 minutes on the counter or up to overnight in the fridge. Remove from fridge 30 minutes before cooking.

Heat a large pan over medium high heat.

Add 2 Tbsp **oil** and marinated chicken. Cook for 7-8 minutes stirring every 2 minutes.

Once chicken pieces are cooked through, remove from the pan and set aside. To the same pan add **onions** (and **jalapeño** if using), remaining 1 Tbsp **oil** and 1 tsp **salt**. Stir to combine. Cook for 20 minutes, stirring often.

Return chicken pieces to the pan, cook for 1 minute stirring the whole time. Once chicken is heated through, add **wine**. Use a wooden spoon to scrape up all the bits from the bottom of the pan. Cook for 2 minutes and then shut off heat and set aside to cool.

Once cooled, preheat oven to 175°C (350°F) and line 2 baking sheets with parchment paper.

In a bowl, combine **mayonnaise**, **schug**, **lemon juice** and **salt**. Set aside or store in an airtight container in the fridge for up 2 weeks.

Roll out **puff pastry**. Cut pastry into 3 inch squares.

Place 1 Tbsp of schug mixture into one corner of the square, leaving a ½ inch border. Using a slotted spoon, remove 1-2 Tbsp chicken mixture (allowing to drain for a moment or two) and place over the schug mixture. Fold boreka over to create a triangle. Use a fork to seal the edges. Place on baking sheet leaving 1 inch between borekas. Repeat until you used all your filling.

Brush the tops with **egg**. Bake for 45 minutes until golden and puffy and beautiful.

Serve hot with a drizzle of techina and enjoy!

lemon herb skillet chicken

IMAGINE YOU'RE MAKING A DINNER OR DISH FOR SHABBOS THAT TOOK YOU SO LITTLE TIME TO PREPARE BUT TASTES AND LOOKS LIKE YOU ORDERED FROM AN UPSCALE RESTAURANT. THAT'S WHAT THIS IS. LEMON IS THE NUMBER ONE MOST LOVED FLAVOR IN MY HOUSE. IT'S EASY TO MAKE, BRIGHT AND SCRUMPTIOUS!

Serves 8

CHICKEN:

12 thin chicken cutlets

6 cloves garlic minced

2 Tbsp olive oil

2 tsp kosher salt

½ tsp pepper

TO COOK:

2-3 Tbsp olive oil

4 cloves garlic, cut into slices

2 lemons, 1 halved, 1 cut into 6 slices

2 Tbsp honey

1½ cup chicken stock

½ tsp kosher salt

½ tsp pepper

6 sprigs parsley

1 sprig thyme

½ sprig rosemary

Feel free to swap out the herbs for any you have or prefer!

Preheat oven to 175°C (350°F).

In a bowl, combine **chicken**, **garlic**, **olive oil**, **salt** and **pepper**.

Heat skillet (or oven safe pan) over medium high heat.

Add **oil** and 3-4 pieces of chicken (make sure not to overcrowd the pan). Working in batches, brown the chicken for 2 minutes on each side. Remove from pan and continue with the rest of the chicken. You may need to add 1-2 more Tbsp of oil between batches.

Once all the chicken is browned add the **garlic**, cook for 30 seconds and then add the juice of 1 **lemon**, **honey**, **chicken stock**, **salt** and **pepper**. Stir, making sure to scrape up any bits from the bottom of the pan. Return chicken to the pan.

Add 3-4 pieces of chicken to the pan, then 1-2 sprigs of the **herbs** and 2 **lemon slices**. Add another layer of chicken and repeat until all the chicken, herbs and lemon have been added.

Spoon some liquid over the top, and cover pan tightly with foil.

Place the pan in the oven and bake for 30 minutes. If your pan is not oven safe, gently transfer everything to a greased baking dish, cover tightly and cook like that.

Serve hot and enjoy!

chicken cacciatore

AN ODE TO ELI. THE FIRST YEAR WE WERE MARRIED, FOR ELI'S BIRTHDAY I ASKED HIM WHAT HE WANTED FOR DINNER. HE SAID "SOMETHING WITH SOFT PIECES OF CHICKEN IN A SAUCY TYPE SITUATION OVER PASTA." OBVIOUSLY HE WAS DESCRIBING THIS ICONIC ITALIAN DISH WITHOUT REALIZING, AND SO I HAD TO MAKE IT. WELL, 17 YEARS LATER, IT'S STILL HIS FAVORITE AND NOW YOU CAN LOVE IT TOO!

Serves 6-8

10 thin chicken cutlets, each piece cut in half horizontally

1 cup flour

3 tsp kosher salt, divided

1 tsp black pepper

1 tsp granulated onion

2 Tbsp olive oil (may need an extra 1-2 tsps)

1 large yellow onion, halved, thinly sliced

1 carrot, peeled, halved lengthwise, thinly sliced

2 zucchini, halved lengthwise, thinly sliced

4 cloves garlic, smashed

1 Calabrian chili (or any chili, you have. Keep in mind the smaller the chili the spicier!)

2 Tbsp capers

1 cup olives, pitted, halved (whatever color you love!)

2 cups kale, stems removed, roughly chopped

½ cup dry red wine

1 (15oz) can tomato sauce

1 cup chicken stock (or water, may need an extra **½ cup** during cooking)

1 lb angel hair pasta

In a bowl combine **chicken**, **flour**, 2 tsp **salt**, **pepper** and **granulated onion**. Mix to coat.

Heat large pan (with a lid is ideal) over medium high heat. Add 1 Tbsp **oil**. Brown chicken in small batches, so as not to overcrowd, for 2 minutes on each side. You may need to add another 1-2 teaspoons **oil** to the pan between batches. Once each piece is browned remove from the pan and set aside.

Add 1 Tbsp **oil** along with **onion** and **carrot**. Cook for 6 minutes stirring often. Add **zucchini**, stir and then cook for 15 minutes only stirring every 6-7 minutes to allow zucchini to slightly caramelize.

Add **garlic**, **chili**, **capers**, **olives** and **kale**. Stir to combine.

Pour in **wine** and use a wooden spoon to scrape up any bits from the bottom of the pan. Cook for 1-2 minutes to allow wine to reduce.

Add **tomato sauce** and **chicken stock**, stir to combine. Bring sauce to a boil. Return chicken to pan making sure each piece is nestled in the sauce.

Lower heat to a gentle simmer, cover tightly and cook fo 1 hour. If it seems like sauce needs more liquid after 30 minutes of cooking, add an additional ½ cup of either stock or water.

Thirty minutes before chicken is done, bring a large pot of **water** to a boil.

Add 2 Tbsp **kosher salt** to the boiling water and angel hair pasta (or whichever pasta you are using). Stir to prevent sticking. Cook until pasta is al dente.

Drain. Place onto a large rimmed platter or bowl.

When the chicken is ready it will be soft and tender and the sauce rich and flavorful! Spoon chicken and sauce gently over pasta and enjoy!

If you want to serve
this at the Shabbos
night meal add 1 tsp
of olive oil to the
pasta after cooking
to prevent sticking.
Heat pasta and
chicken separately
and then combine
just before serving.

sticky chicken pastrami hash

WE ALL NEED A DISH THAT'S JUST A CROWD PLEASER. THE TYPE OF THING THAT'S VERSATILE (SWAP, ADD, CHANGE) AND QUICK TO THROW TOGETHER. THAT'S WHAT THIS IS. THE FLAVORS ARE APPROACHABLE, LIKED BY BASICALLY EVERYONE (I HAVE YET TO SERVE THIS TO ANYONE WHO TURNED IT DOWN) AND HAS INGREDIENTS USUALLY FOUND IN YOUR HOUSE. PLUS, IT CAN BE SERVED IN SO MANY DIFFERENT WAYS SO YOU CAN KEEP MAKING IT WITHOUT IT EVER BECOMING HUMDRUM!

Serves 6

12 thin chicken cutlets, sliced into ½ inch strips

6 tsp neutral oil, divided

1 tsp kosher salt, divided

1 tsp black pepper

1 tsp paprika

2 tsp granulated onion

1 tsp granulated garlic

12 oz (240 g) pastrami, cut into ¼ inch strips

1 large yellow onion, diced

1 jalapeño, thinly sliced (optional)

¾ cup duck sauce (original flavor)

In a small bowl, combine **chicken**, 2 tsp **oil**, ½ tsp **salt**, **pepper**, **paprika**, **granulated onion** and **granulated garlic**. Stir to coat chicken pieces evenly. Set aside.

Heat a large pan over medium high heat.

Add 2 tsp **oil** and **pastrami**. Cook, stirring often, for about 10-12 minutes until pastrami pieces are crispy. Use a slotted spoon to remove pastrami (leaving oil in the pan) to a bowl and set aside.

Add **onion** and **jalapeño** (if using) and remaining **salt** to the pan. Cook for 10-12 minutes, stirring often. Add cooked onion and jalapeño to the bowl with the cooked pastrami and set aside.

Add remaining 1 tsp **oil** and all the chicken to the pan. Cook for 5-6 minutes, stirring often, until all the chicken is cooked through.

Return pastrami, onions and jalapeños to the pan. Stir to combine.

Pour in **duck sauce** and stir to coat everything. Once the sauce starts to bubble, remove from heat.

Serve hash hot, over rice, in a wrap, baguette or pita or even over a baked potato!

chicken and broccoli

CHINESE FOOD.
MAKE IT. THAT'S THE REASON.
YOU'RE WELCOME.
ALSO, PUT SOME AWAY AND EAT IT COLD RIGHT OUT OF THE FRIDGE.

Serves 6-8

TO VELVET:

10 thin chicken cutlets, cut into ¼ inch pieces

3 Tbsp cold water

2 tsp soy sauce

2 tsp cornstarch

2 tsp neutral oil

TO COOK:

2 Tbsp neutral oil, divided

1 scant tsp sesame oil

6 cloves garlic, minced

½ inch piece ginger, grated

1 (32 oz) bag frozen broccoli, defrosted completely, stems removed

1 can baby corn, drained, cut into 1 inch pieces

1 cup low sodium soy sauce, divided

⅔ cup sugar

2-3 tsp crushed red pepper flakes (or less if you don't like it spicy)

2 Tbsp cornstarch, dissolved in **2 Tbsp** water

3-4 scallions, thinly sliced

Place **chicken** pieces in a medium sized bowl. Add **water** and **soy sauce**. Use your hands to mix well and massage liquid into the chicken. Set aside for 5-10 minutes. Add **cornstarch** and **oil**. Mix well to make sure all the pieces are lightly coated. Set aside for 15-20 minutes.

Heat a very large pan over medium high heat, add 1 Tbsp **neutral oil**, **sesame oil**, **garlic** and **ginger** and stir for 30 seconds.

Add in the chicken pieces using a slotted spoon or your hands so that you don't add any juices that may have accumulated in the bowl. Cook chicken pieces for 10-12 minutes stirring every 2 minutes or so.

Add remaining **neutral oil**, **broccoli**, **baby corn** and ½ cup **soy sauce**, stir gently to combine. Cook for 8-10 minutes, stirring often, until veggies are heated through.

Add remaining **soy sauce**, **sugar** and **red pepper flakes** to the pan and stir to combine. Bring to a boil add dissolved **cornstarch** to the pan and stir. Allow sauce to boil for 1 minute, then shut off heat, add **scallions**, serve hot over rice and enjoy!

sheet pan dijon chicken and potatoes

A DINNER ON A PAN. A COMPLETE MEAL THAT IS ACTUALLY STILL MOIST AND JUICY AND PACKED WITH FLAVOR.

Serves 6

8 boneless, skinless chicken thighs

2 shallots, peeled, halved, thinly sliced

½ kilo (1 lb) baby red potatoes, washed, halved (about 12-15)

MARINADE:

4 Tbsp tomato paste

4 Tbsp dijon mustard

3 Tbsp olive oil

1 large lemon, juiced (about ¼ cup)

1 Tbsp kosher salt

½ tsp dried rosemary

½ tsp dried thyme

1 tsp crushed red pepper flakes

5 cloves garlic, minced

Preheat oven to 200°C (400°F) and line a baking sheet with parchment paper.

Place **chicken**, **shallots** and **potatoes** on the baking sheet.

In a small bowl, add **all the marinade ingredients** and mix well to combine. Pour marinade over everything on the baking sheet. Use your hands to rub marinade all over the chicken and potatoes.

Spread everything on the sheet pan in a single layer. Place baking sheet, uncovered, in the oven for 1 hour. Remove baking sheet from the oven, serve hot and enjoy!

REPURPOSE: This dish is delicious turned into a salad right when cooked or repurposed if there are leftovers. I like to prepare a large bowl with arugula, or any other greens I have on hand, some kalamata olives and whatever crunchy vegetables I have in my fridge. Lay the roasted potatoes and chicken right over the salad and serve!

one pot chicken and ptitim

I USUALLY DEFROST MY CHICKEN THE NIGHT BEFORE AND REALLY HAVE NO IDEA WHAT I PLAN TO MAKE FOR DINNER, ONLY THAT IT WILL INCLUDE CHICKEN. THE NEXT DAY COMES AND LIFE HAPPENS AND COME FIVE PM I STILL HAVE NOT GIVEN DINNER ANY THOUGHT. AT THIS POINT EVERYONE IS HUNGRY, ABOUT TO TURN THE CORNER TO CRANKY, I HAVE CHICKEN DEFROSTED AND NEED DINNER TO BE DELICIOUS AND ON THE TABLE QUICKLY. ENTER CHICKEN AND PTITIM.

Serves 4-6

6 thin chicken cutlets, cut into ¼ inch strips

3 Tbsp olive oil, divided

1 yellow onion, halved, thinly sliced

1½ tsp granulated onion

1½ tsp granulated garlic

½ tsp turmeric

1 tsp kosher salt

½ tsp black pepper

3¼ cups (500 g) ptitim (Israeli couscous)

3⅓ cups chicken stock (leftover chicken soup/ chicken soup mix dissolved in water/stock in a box...)

½ cup parsley leaves, chopped (optional)

If you want to add a little pep in your step, try adding one thinly sliced jalapeño to the pot along with the onions!

Heat a medium sized pot (that has a cover) over medium high heat.

Add 1 Tbsp **oil** and **onion** and cook for 15 minutes, stirring often.

Once onion browns, move it to the sides of the pot, add 1 Tbsp **oil** and **chicken** to the center. Before stirring sprinkle the **seasoning** over the chicken. Stir to combine everything together, including the onions. Cook for 5 minutes, stirring often, until chicken is cooked through.

Add remaining **oil** to the pot along with all the **ptitim**. Stir constantly for 4-5 minutes until some of the ptitim start to slightly darken in color.

Add in the **stock**. Bring mixture to a boil, then reduce heat to low, cover the pot, and allow to simmer for 10-12 minutes.

Remove cover, gently stir, shut off the heat and cover again for 4 minutes to continue steaming.

If using, sprinkle **parsley** over the top, serve hot and enjoy!

My kids favorite way to eat this is by drizzling techina and dolloping schug over their bowls!

general tso chicken

STOP. BEFORE YOU TURN THE PAGE JUST HEAR ME OUT. IT'S LONG, YOU HAVE TO FRY THE CHICKEN TWICE, AND IT'S, WELL, IT'S A PATCHKE. I SAID IT. IT'S TRUE AND IT'S NOT EMBARRASSED ABOUT HOW NEEDY IT IS AND THAT'S BECAUSE IT IS WORTH IT. MAKE IT AND YOU WILL BE REWARDED WITH THE BEST GENERAL TSO CHICKEN EVER!

Serves 12

CHICKEN:

2.3 kilo (5 lb) chicken cutlets, cut into ½ inch strips
1 tsp kosher salt
1 tsp pepper
6 cloves garlic, minced
2 cups rice flour
1 cup cornstarch
2 eggs, beaten
2 Tbsp soy sauce
1 cup seltzer
neutral oil, for frying

SAUCE:

1 tsp neutral oil
1 tsp sesame oil
5 cloves garlic, minced
½ inch piece ginger, minced
1 cup soy sauce
1 cup honey
2 Tbsp seasoned rice vinegar
1 cup hoisin sauce
1 Tbsp cornstarch dissolved in **2 Tbsp** water
1-2 Tbsp crushed red pepper flakes (optional)
2 scallions, thinly sliced, for garnish
1-2 tsp sesame seeds, for garnish

In a large bowl, add **chicken**, **salt**, **pepper**, **garlic**, **rice flour** and **cornstarch**. Beat **eggs** and **soy souce** together, add to the bowl with the chicken. Add **seltzer**. Mix. Set aside for 20-30 minutes.

Meanwhile, fill a large pot halfway with **oil** and heat over medium high heat.

While the oil is heating up, make the sauce. In a medium pot add **oils**, **garlic** and **ginger**. Cook, stirring often, for 3 minutes. Once fragrant add in **soy sauce**, **honey**, **rice vinegar**, **hoisin sauce** and **red pepper flakes** (if using). Bring to a boil.

Add **cornstarch mixture**. Stir. Bring sauce back to a boil, and cook for 1-2 minutes stirring constantly so that the sauce can thicken. Set aside while you cook chicken.

Place a cooling rack over a piece of parchment paper next to your stove.

When the oil is hot, fry chicken in small batches for 2-3 minutes then remove and drain on prepared cooling rack. Chicken will be light in color and not crunchy.

Once all the chicken is cooked fry the pieces a second time in small batches for 3-4 minutes until golden and crispy.

Reheat sauce and pour over chicken. Toss to make sure every piece is coated in the sticky goodness.

Sprinkle as much **red pepper flakes**, **scallions** and **sesame seeds** as you like. Serve and enjoy!

BONUS TIP: There's nothing more appealing than a fridge with leftover Chinese food! Put some in a small container in the fridge so you have cold Chinese food on hand for all late night snackings!

COOK THE BOOK

scan QR code to cook
the recipes in this book
alongside Danielle